COSTUME AROUND THE WORLD
India

Kathy Elgin

CHELSEA
CLUBHOUSE
An Imprint of Chelsea House Publishers

Copyright © 2008 Bailey Publishing Associates Ltd

Produced for Chelsea Clubhouse by Bailey Publishing Associates Ltd
11a Woodlands, Hove BN3 6TJ
England

Project Manager: Roberta Bailey
Editor: Alex Woolf
Text Designer: Jane Hawkins
Picture Research: Roberta Bailey and Shelley Noronha

Chelsea Clubhouse
An imprint of Chelsea House Publishers
132 West 31st Street
New York NY 10001

ISBN 978-0-7910-9768-7

Library of Congress Cataloging-in-Publication Data
Costume around the world.—1st ed.
     v. cm.
     Includes bibliographical references and index.
     Contents: [1] China / Anne Rooney—[2] France / Kathy Elgin—[3] Germany / Cath Senker—[4] India / Kathy Elgin—[5] Italy / Kathy Elgin—[6] Japan / Jane Bingham—[7] Mexico / Jane Bingham—[8] Saudi Arabia / Cath Senker—[9] Spain / Kathy Elgin—[10] United States / Liz Gogerly.
     ISBN 978-0-7910-9765-6 (v. 1)—ISBN 978-0-7910-9766-3 (v. 2)—ISBN 978-0-7910-9767-0 (v. 3)—ISBN 978-0-7910-9768-7 (v. 4)—ISBN 978-0-7910-9769-4 (v. 5)—ISBN 978-0-7910-9770-0 (v. 6)—ISBN 978-0-7910-9771-7 (v. 7)—ISBN 978-0-7910-9773-1 (v. 8)— ISBN 978-0-7910-9772-4 (v. 9)—ISBN 978-0-7910-9774-8 (v. 10) 1. Clothing and dress—Juvenile literature.
     GT518.C67 2008
     391—dc22   2007042756

Printed and bound in Hong Kong

10 9 8 7 6 5 4 3 2 1

The publishers would like to thank the following for permission to reproduce their pictures:
Chris Fairclough Worldwide Ltd: 6, 12, 14 and title page, 24
Dinodia: 5, 27
Topfoto: 4(Hal Beral), 7(British Museum/HIP), 8(Sean Sprague/Image Works), 10, 11 (Spectrum Colour Library/HIP), 15 (Macduff Everton/Image Works), 16(DPA/AA/Image Works), 17, 20 (Hal Beral), 21(UPP), 23(Christine Pemberton/Image Works), 25(Hal Beral), 26, 28, 29 (ACNational Pictures)
www.cbazaar.com: 18, 19

Contents

India's Colorful Culture

Indian civilization is one of the oldest in the world, dating back over 4,000 years. Since then, immigrants and invaders have added their own traditions. Today's India has a rich and varied culture. There is a strong British influence, because Britain ruled India for almost 200 years, until 1947.

The streets of India are thronged with people wearing a variety of styles and colors.

India is made up of 28 states, from Rajastan in the north to Tamil Nadu at the southern tip. Each has its own traditions, costumes, and languages. Despite the recent technological revolution, India

is still largely a rural country. There is a big gap between rich and poor, town and country. Clothing is often an indication of this. Workers in poor farming villages may have only one or two simple cotton outfits, made by the local tailor. Rich people can afford store-bought silk saris and imported clothes.

Signs of status

Indian women take clothes very seriously. They love color and fine fabrics. Even the poor take care to dress as well as they can afford to. An Indian can usually tell just by looking at another Indian person's clothes how rich they are, which state they come from, how important their job is, and which religion they follow.

Like young people all over the world, India's younger generation enjoys Western-style clothes, especially American jeans and T-shirts. Many of these are made in India and exported to America!

The word on the streets

Many words connected with clothing come from Indian languages. *Pajamas* comes from *pai* (leg) and *jamah* (garment). *Dungarees* comes from *dungri* (the coarse cloth these pants were made from), and *bandanna* from *badhnu* (tie-dyed). *Khaki* is the Indian word for "dust colored," and *cashmere* comes from Kashmir, where it was first produced.

Sonia Gandhi, a prominent politician, is Italian, but when she married the late prime minister Rajiv Gandhi, she wore saris to identify with her new country.

From Desert to Downpour

The Indian subcontinent stretches from the snow-covered Himalayan mountains in the northeast to the tropical southern tip. Over a distance of 3,500 miles (5,635 kilometers), the climate varies greatly.

Fishermen on the coast of Kerala, in the south, wear cool cotton clothing.

The eastern state of Meghalaya gets more rainfall than anywhere in the world. In the northwest is the Thar Desert, the driest place on earth. Here, the women wear brilliantly colored skirts and the men, impressive turbans.

originally the costume of the Punjab region. When part of Punjab became the new Islamic country of Pakistan in 1947, the costume became associated with Islam. Sikhs also came originally from this region. They are easily recognized by their turbans. Buddhist monks are identified by their saffron yellow robes.

Dance costume

Dance theater is important in Indian culture. It began in temples and usually tells stories of the gods. Kathak, from the north, is an energetic storytelling dance performed by men and women wearing long flared dresses and ankle bells. Only women can dance Bharata Natyam, swaying and making subtle hand movements. For this graceful dance, they wear a pleated skirt, which opens like a fan, and jewelry, bells, and flowers.

Kathakali dance is performed only by men. Their elaborate makeup, representing demons and heroes, transforms the face into a mask.

Soft Silk and Cool Cotton

India's main textiles are cotton, which grows there naturally, and silk, which was introduced from China. Cheap cottons and artificial silks are mass-produced, but the most highly prized fabrics are those woven by hand.

Cotton is worn everywhere but especially in the country and by the working class. The best cotton clothing is made in the villages by local craftsmen who use traditional techniques. They color homespun fabrics with vegetable dyes and use a variety of decorative printing styles. Chennai is especially famous for its checked cottons, known as madras cotton from the city's old name. This design developed as an imitation of the tartans worn by Scottish soldiers based there in the 19th century.

Block printing is a skilled trade. The pattern blocks have to be carefully positioned to get the repeat pattern right.

The naked princess

A Bengali legend tells that Princess Zebunissa, the daughter of Emperor Aurangzeb (1618–1707), once shocked her father by appearing naked in public. In fact, she was wearing a dress made of cotton-muslin so fine that although it was wrapped seven times around her body, it was almost transparent.

These dancing girls are wearing semitransparent muslin skirts and tunics over their close-fitting pants.

Traditional techniques

Better-off women, who have a choice, wear cotton saris in summer and silk in winter. Silk is much more expensive and is usually made by professionals. Although it is produced all over India, the most famous silk towns are Kanchipuram and Varanasi. Here, hundreds of small family businesses continue to produce traditional silk saris on hand looms. These saris are worn for weddings and special occasions.

Wool from sheep and goats is used in the cooler northern regions for shawls and waistcoats. These natural fabrics are beautiful. However, some people prefer nylon drip-dry shirts and chiffon saris, which are easier to wash and dry.

Dressing for the Occasion

Weddings are big occasions. Celebrations last for several days, with a change of clothes for each day. Even modern couples wear traditional outfits for their marriage.

For the ceremony, the bride wears a red silk sari thickly embroidered with gold thread. This symbolizes fertility and good fortune. She is weighed down with gold jewelry. Most bridegrooms wear a traditional north Indian *sherwani* coat and *churidar* pants (see page 18).

Brides receive a whole new wardrobe of saris from their husband's family. The exchange of saris as gifts

The art of embroidery

Zardosi is hand embroidery with gold or silver threads on velvet or heavy silk. *Kasooti*, from Karnataka, is a delicate style worked on silk. In Rajastan, tiny mirrors are stitched into the pattern to reflect light. *Chikankari*, from Uttar Pradesh, is white thread embroidery on white fabric. Crewelwork, from Kashmir, has chain-stitch patterns worked in wool or silk.

Appliqué—sewing cutout patterns onto fabric—is a popular kind of embroidery.

between other relatives is also important. Weddings can be very expensive.

The bride and groom are elaborately dressed for the main ceremony.

Mourning clothes

White is the color of mourning and funerals. In many parts of India, widows are expected to wear a white sari for the rest of their lives. This is a sign that "color" and happiness have gone from their lives.

Festival costume

Throughout the year, there are ceremonies celebrating spring, harvest time, and various gods or legendary heroes. For Vasant Panchami, in February, people wear yellow to welcome spring. For the festival of Diwali, in November, people buy new clothes in honor of the goddess Lakshmi. The lighthearted festival of Holi, however, is quite different. People throw colored powder over each other, so of course they wear their oldest clothes.

The Peacock Male

Until recently, many Indian men preferred Western clothes. Today they are rediscovering the elegant outfits of earlier times. Like their ancestors, today's Indian men are not afraid to wear elaborate fabrics, embroidery, and bright colors.

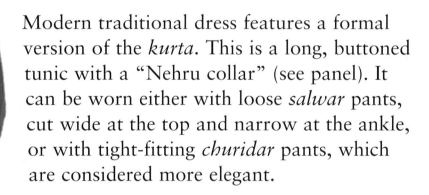

Modern traditional dress features a formal version of the *kurta*. This is a long, buttoned tunic with a "Nehru collar" (see panel). It can be worn either with loose *salwar* pants, cut wide at the top and narrow at the ankle, or with tight-fitting *churidar* pants, which are considered more elegant.

Over this goes a *sherwani*, a long, close-fitting coat first worn at the Mughal court in the 16th century. A long scarf, usually with a decorative border, hangs over one shoulder. This style originated in northern India but is now popular all over the country, especially for weddings. The *sherwani* can be made of fine wool, silk, or brocade and is often embroidered.

The *sherwani* coat makes almost any man look smart. No wonder—it was what emperors wore.

18

East meets West

An alternative is the *jodhpuri*, or "prince suit," which mixes Indian and Western styles. A buttonless jacket, shorter than the *sherwani* but also with a Nehru collar, is worn with an embroidered tunic and Western-style pants.

Stylish shoes or more traditional embroidered leather slippers are worn with these suits. Even men who prefer to wear Armani or Hugo Boss like to add a traditional touch. This could be an embroidered silk waistcoat, a silk tie, or a scarf.

The *jodhpuri* suit is a symbol of modern India, poised between East and West.

From politics to pop

The "Nehru collar" is a stand-up collar band named after the first prime minister of India, Jawaharlal Nehru (1880–1964), who liked to wear this traditional style. In the 1960s, "Nehru jackets" were given worldwide popularity by the Beatles, who wore them on their 1968 trip to India.

Sari or Shalwar?

Unlike men, Indian women never abandoned their traditional clothing for Western fashions. They stuck to their regional styles. Dressing up now means a much wider choice. They can wear a sari, a *shalwar kameez* outfit, or a designer dress, depending on the occasion.

The *shalwar kameez*, sometimes called a "suit," is no longer associated only with Muslims. International designers have made it a high-fashion garment. Young women consider it more "modern" than the sari. It is also easier to manage. The *dupatta*, or long scarf, used to be worn across the chest as a symbol of modesty. Today it is thrown over one shoulder as a decorative touch.

Fads and fashions

For many, however, the sari is more elegant. Its graceful folds show off a slim figure better

Different generations of the same family might choose to wear a sari or a *shalwar kameez*, while children love Western clothes.

than a suit. The "Nivi" style, with the *pallu* (the decorated end of the sari) thrown over the left shoulder, is the most popular. However, different regional styles go in and out of style. Fashion-conscious girls make sure they know how to tie all of them and which fabric suits each style.

Indians are good at giving traditional garments a new twist. Great attention is paid to detail. The length of the *choli* sleeve (see page 6) or how the *pallu* is draped makes all the difference. Many women own hundreds of saris in different fabrics for summer and winter, formal and casual.

Even fashion-conscious girls know how to starch a sari using the water left over from cooking rice!

Bangles around your ankles

The tight-fitting pants worn by both men and women are called *churidar*. This comes from the words *dar* (like) and *churi* (bangle). The long pants fall into folds, which look like a set of bangles resting on the ankle. This matches the set of bangles women wear on their arms.

Looking Good at Work

Farmers, especially in the south, work hard in the fields using buffalo and oxen. Work clothing is usually just a white or checked cotton shirt and either a *lungi* or shorts. Fishermen on the coast and canals of Kerala, in southwest India on the Arabian Sea, often wear only a kind of loincloth.

Women also work in the fields. The sari is a versatile working garment. It can be tucked up to make movement easier or pulled over the head as shelter from the heat. Working mothers even carry babies wrapped into its folds.

School uniforms

Young children wear school uniforms based on the English-style pinafore and blouse or shirt and shorts. Since the 1980s, many schools have adopted *shalwar-kameez*-style uniforms for older girls ages 12 to 16. This is considered more modest than short skirts. It is also more practical than a sari for riding a bike, playing games, and sports, so girls have more freedom.

Working in the rice fields of Goa is no place for fashion.

Military and police

The uniforms of the military and the police are based on those of the British forces. The army wears khaki; the navy, dark blue; and the airforce, light blue. Indian police wear khaki shirts and pants with a white lanyard and a peaked cap. Indians take their responsibilities seriously and are proud of their uniforms. They always look stylish, in spite of the heat.

These schoolgirls, whether Muslim or Hindu, all wear the same *shalwar kameez* uniform.

Sweet-smelling uniforms

In 2007, the state of Gujarat made world headlines by introducing new uniforms for the police force. They were made of lightweight material and specially treated with rose or lemon fragrance to make them smell better in the summer heat. The high-tech fabric also glowed in the dark. The authorities hoped that this would reduce the number of traffic accidents.

Relaxing in Style

Traditional leisurewear in India is similar to formal clothing, but in less expensive material. Cotton or artificial fabrics replace silk saris for relaxing around the house.

It's quite common to see whole families traveling in style on a motorcycle or scooter.

Women who wear the sari outdoors often wear a *shalwar kameez* for comfort in the privacy of their own home. Teenage girls in particular, who still find a sari difficult to manage, prefer to relax in a "suit."

Another alternative is the "maxi," a grown-up version of the simple long dress worn by little girls. Maxis are worn inside the home and sometimes outside. A village woman might also wear a gathered skirt and buttoned blouse.

Smart casual

Casual clothing for many young Indian men, especially in northern India, means jeans, T-shirts, and baseball caps. Those from more traditional families wear a *kurta* pajama. This is a long shirt, worn with either loose or *churidar* pants. Indian society is quite formal. Even in casual dress, it is considered rude to speak to someone with your sari or dhoti tucked up.

Sporting styles

Indians are wild about sports, especially cricket and hockey. Both national teams wear high-tech Nike outfits in pale blue. Soccer is less popular. In 1950, the national soccer team withdrew from competition because the players refused to wear boots. Now that women have the modesty of the *shalwar kameez*, more of them are taking up sports. But even in saris, girls go swimming.

Perfect for housework

The *pallu* of an everyday sari is very versatile. It is used to cover the head, to hide the face from strangers, for wiping sweat, or for cleaning children's faces. It also serves as an oven mitt or a duster and for carrying harvested crops in the fields. In Bengal, it is traditional for a wife to tie her *pallu* to her husband's dhoti on their wedding night.

This street vendor is wearing the everyday *kurta* pajama in pale cotton.

25

Henna, Bangles, and Beads

Indian women still use traditional cosmetics as well as commercial ones. They darken their eyelids and lashes with kohl, made from soot. Henna, or *mehndi*, is a brown paste used to paint designs on a woman's hands and feet.

Legend says the first to use henna was Mumtaz Mahal, in whose memory the Taj Mahal was built.

It used to be the only form of decoration for village women who could not afford jewelry. Today it is very fashionable and always worn for weddings. *Bindis* are colored spots applied to the forehead. The color is chosen to match the sari.

Henna for happiness

Mehndi (or henna) designs vary between regions. They symbolize good luck and fertility. On the *mehndi raat* (henna night) before the wedding, the bride's girlfriends spend hours telling stories, drinking tea, and eating sweets as they paint her hands and feet. Traditionally, brides do not have to do any work until the henna wears off.

Jewelry

All Indian women wear bangles—either expensive gold ones or heaps of glittering colored glass ones from the bazaar. A woman's gold jewelry is far more than something pretty to wear—it is her financial security. Girls are given their own jewelry when they get married. It is quite usual for men to wear gold bracelets, rings, and neck chains too. Traditional tribal jewelry is made of silver and semiprecious beads in ancient designs. Nose rings, anklets, and toe rings are also worn.

Traditionally, Indians did not wear underwear and slept in a plain version of their day clothes. These days, Western-style lingerie and nightclothes are popular but in Indian patterns.

In India, there's no such thing as too much gold jewelry. Most Indian jewelry is based on traditional designs.

Hairstyles

Most women wear their hair long, either in a simple braid or pinned up. Men prefer short hair and mustaches but rarely beards. Sikhs are the exception. They are not allowed to cut their hair. They conceal their long hair inside the turban but are easily recognized by their beards.

India Goes International

Colonists introduced European clothing to India and took Indian textiles back to their own countries. A flower-printed fabric called chintz was all the rage in 18th-century England. French travelers took the technique of block printing on cotton back to Provence in the south of France. The fabric industry they started is still flourishing there today.

All over the United States, hippies who had traveled in India set up boutiques selling imported clothing.

Later, Scottish soldiers took home fine wool shawls with a particular swirly pattern. They were copied in the Scottish town of Paisley and became known as paisley shawls. They were the height of fashion in the Victorian period.

Trendsetters

In the 1960s, hippies all over America wore *kurtas*, Nehru jackets, and beads with their flared jeans. Women wore dresses made out of sari fabric, silver bangles, and long, dangling earrings. More recently, designers such as Ralph Lauren and Tommy Hilfiger have made madras checked shirts and shorts popular all over again.

Today Indian style is high fashion. Princess Diana, Hillary Clinton, and Jemima Khan, a British socialite, were the first Western women to promote the *shalwar kameez*. It was soon being copied by top fashion designers. Hollywood stars now wear *bindis* and henna on their hands instead of tattoos. The height of celebrity chic is an Indian-style wedding. The Indian film industry, known as Bollywood, has also boosted Indian fashion, thanks to its glamorous costumes. However, not many Westerners are brave enough yet to wear a sari.

Warm and woolly

The fashion essential of the 1990s was the pashmina. This soft, warm shawl is made from the fine hair combed from the underfleece of a mountain goat. Pashminas can be plain or paisley patterned, but all have a knotted fringe. Traditionally, they are fine enough to pull through a wedding ring.

Bollywood star Shilpa Shetty and her sister Shamita show off some cutting-edge Indian fashion.

Glossary

Bharata Natyam An ancient southern Indian dance performed in temple and court.

bindi A teardrop-shaped decoration applied to the forehead.

block printing Printing a repeat pattern using a design carved from a block of wood.

brocade A richly decorative woven fabric.

Buddhist A follower of a religion based on the teachings of the Buddha.

chikankari White embroidery, also known as shadow work.

choli A short, fitted blouse worn under the sari.

churidar Close-fitting pants that fall in folds to the ankle.

dhoti A draped garment worn by men around the lower part of the body.

Diwali The Hindu festival of lights.

dupatta A long scarf worn with the *shalwar kameez*, draped around both shoulders and hanging down across the chest.

export A product sold to another country.

Hinduism The main religion of India.

Holi The Hindu spring festival, also called the festival of colors.

Islam A religion founded in the seventh century CE, by the prophet Mohammed, and based on obedience to Allah.

Jain A follower of an ancient religion that preaches a life of harmlessness and renunciation.

kameez A long, loose tunic.

kasooti A fine embroidery worked on silk fabric, usually in a geometric design.

kohl An eye cosmetic made by mixing soot with oil or grease.

kurta A somewhat fitted tunic.

kurta pajama A tunic-and-pants outfit.

Lakshmi The Hindu goddess of wealth, light, and wisdom.

lanyard A cord worn around the neck to hold a whistle.

lungi A men's garment, similar to a sarong.

maxi A simple, long frock, usually with a frilled bodice.

missionary A religious teacher sent to a foreign country to convert the population.

monsoon The period of heavy rainfall in India, between June and October.

mosque A Muslim place of worship.

Mughals Muslims from the Middle East who brought Persian culture to India in the 16th century.

muslin A very fine, almost transparent cotton fabric.

Nehru collar A stand-up collar band made popular by Prime Minister Nehru.

pallu The decorated end of the sari, usually draped over the shoulder.

Parvati The mother goddess, wife of Lord Shiva.

sari A woman's draped garment, made of 16 feet (5 meters) of cloth.

shalwar Baggy pants tied at the waist and narrowing to the ankle.

sherwani A long, close-fitting coat, first worn at the Mughal court.

Sikh A follower of the religion founded in the 16th century by Guru Nanak.

subcontinent A large landmass that is part of a larger continent.

turban A head covering made by winding a long strip of cloth around the head.

Further Information

Books

Chatterjee, Manini. *Eyewitness Books: India*. Dorling Kindersley, 2002.

Conboy, Fiona. *Welcome to My Country: India*. Gareth Stevens, 2000.

Dalal, Anita. *Nations of the World: India*. Raintree, 2003.

Landau, Elaine. *True Books: India*. Children's Press, 1999.

Parker, Victoria. *We're from India*. Heinemann Library, 2005.

Web sites

www.webindia123.com/india
Information about India, including a section on costume.

www.welcometoindia.com
General information about the country and its people.

www.dollsofindia.com
A Web site devoted to Indian costume, fabrics, and regional costume dolls.

www.iloveindia.com
Information on all aspects of Indian culture.

www.tigersfeet.com
Information about India, including a photo gallery.